From the Heart of Devon

Countryside Garden to Kitchen

Merle Warner

Sparrowhawk

Orchard Books

Dedication

This book is an appreciation of the natural life around us here in Tedburn St Mary, Devon, as well as recipes which I have collected over the last 50 years. They are all favourites, tried and tested and guaranteed to be successful even to the novice cook. It is not a comprehensive cookery book – I do not use a great number of herbs, or any garlic. These can be added to your own taste.

Compiling this book has given me so much pleasure. I dedicate it to my dear husband Raymond upon whose suggestion and with whose encouragement it was written. I must also thank all of my family, each in their own way have contributed.

ISBN 978 1898964 75 9

Published by Orchard

Orchard is an imprint of Tor Mark,
United Downs Ind. Est., St Day, Redruth TR16 5HY

© Merle Warner

First published 2006, this revised edition 2014

Printed by Hedgerow Print, Crediton, Devon EX17 1ES
www.hedgerowprint.co.uk

January

It is New Year's Day and as I open the kitchen door he is there — our robin 'Bobby Dick', as we affectionately call him. He is one of the many birds who come to our bird table and this year they seem to be extra hungry. We have our favourites — there is a cheeky little coal-tit who dashes in and takes a quick peck whenever the opportunity comes. The nuthatch clears the table when he zooms in with his spear like beak — no-one will face him. There are blue-tits, sparrows and blackbirds. We have a special blackbird who we call 'the vicar'. He has been with us several years now, so called because he has a white collar around his throat. They are all a joy to watch but the highlight of the day is when we are graced with the arrival of the spotted woodpecker. He hangs on the peanut holder displaying his beautiful plumage.

Robin

We have many seagulls around at the moment. They do say that they make their way inland when the weather is bad out at sea.

Now is the time to take a walk around the garden. Things look very bleak and cold at this time of the year but on closer inspection it is surprising how many flowers we can find. The brightly coloured yellow jasmine seems to go on flowering for weeks; the winter heathers, pink and white; the sweetly scented mahonia, or as I like to call it 'the lily of the valley tree'; the Christmas roses and the delicate mauve iris stylosa hiding amongst the untidy foliage. The first violets and snowdrops are always special favourites. The robin is still singing to us. He is always here, either in the tall tree or on the bird table. Maybe January is not such a dead month in the garden after all and Spring is not far away.

Woodpecker

Jasmine

We pruned the horse chestnut tree and now have a lovely bunch of sticky buds in a vase of water indoors. They will take some time to open, but will eventually reveal their lovely grey-green foliage, a welcome sight on dark days.

I have noticed a beautiful song thrush in the garden today — we always know when he's around by the evidence of broken snail shells.

January recipes

We think now of what we can have as a winter warmer — meals need to be hot and nourishing, so we think of stews, soups and casseroles. Here is a casserole recipe which can be so useful at busy times. Prepare, put in the oven and then forget it until 15 mins before mealtime.

DOUGHBOY WINTER WARMER

450g (1lb) cubed stewing steak
1 chopped onion   1 tablespoon oil
mixed vegetables; diced carrot, swede, mushroom, parsnip, tomato
vegetable stock or stock cube   gravy thickening

For dumplings;   170g (6oz) self-raising flour
50g (2oz) suet   little cold water

Fry the onion in oil, then brown the stewing steak; put both into a casserole dish, adding the vegetables. Pour on stock to comfortably cover the vegetables. Cover and put into oven 200c, gas mark 6, until simmering. Reduce heat and keep simmering for 2-3 hours.

Before serving add gravy thickening. Mix flour and suet together with cold water and roll into balls. Add to casserole after thickening. Cook for further 15 minutes.

SHEPHERD'S PIE

450g (1lb) minced lamb (or minced beef)
1 tablespoon oil
1 chopped onion
150ml (1/4 pt) stock
1 tablespoon Worcester sauce
2 chopped tomatoes
800g (1lb 12oz) floury potatoes
3 tablespoons milk   25g (1oz) butter
salt and pepper   herbs

Cook potatoes until soft and mash with milk and butter, salt and pepper to taste. Fry the chopped onion in oil; add minced lamb (or beef) and cook for a further 5-6 mins. Stir in the stock, Worcester sauce, tomatoes, herbs, salt and pepper. Simmer for a further 5 mins.

Spoon into a greased ovenproof dish. Cover with mashed potato, spreading right to the edges. Fluff up the surface with a fork, then dot with butter or margarine.

Bake for 35-40 mins, oven 180c, gas mark 4, until golden brown. Serve with fresh vegetables.

Violet

A s January progresses we see Seville oranges in the shops. They remind us it's marmalade making time again. This is a recipe I have used for many years, which I found very reliable.

SEVILLE ORANGE MARMALADE

675g (1 1/2 lbs) Seville oranges   1 lemon
1.4kg (3lbs) sugar   1.7 litres (3pts) cold water

Wash fruit, peel, remove all pith and pips (tie these in a muslin bag). Cut peel into thin shreds* and add to fruit and juice in a large bowl, and the bag of pith and pips. Add 1.7 litres (3 pints) cold water, cover and leave overnight.

The next day turn mixture into a large pan, bring to the boil and simmer gently for 2 1/2 hours until peel is soft and liquid much reduced. Remove bag of pips, squeezing as much liquid as you can from it. Stir in the sugar and when dissolved bring back to a fast boil, boiling hard for 15-20 mins or until the mixture sets when tested on a cold plate. Stand for 10 mins before potting. Cover when cold.

> * Cutting up the peel is very time consuming and good results can be reached by mincing instead, but the appearance is not so pleasing.

THREE FRUIT MARMALADE

1 grapefruit   1 lemon
4 Seville oranges (approx. 675g 1 1/2 lbs fruit in total)
1.4kg (3lbs) sugar   1.7 litres (3pts) cold water

> * Method as for Seville Orange Marmalade.

February

Traditionally February in Devon is a wet month – 'February fill dyke' – and we shall be pleased to see some rain to help refill our well which provides water to the house. We have been very concerned, as up to mid January it was less than a quarter full. Normally it would be full at this time of the year. It is 30 feet deep. According to Devonians it needs bad weather to activate the spring which supplies it and so far this winter it has been quite dry.

Catkins

The geese have our attention at the moment, we have a trio – two geese and a gander. Hannah, Nixie and Hatherleigh. Hatherleigh is the gander's name because he came from the market there. We have them to keep the grass in the orchard under control and they are also excellent guard dogs. We have sunk an old bath in the ground, and when it is refilled the fun they have playing in it is a pleasure to watch. Hannah has just laid her first egg this year, so we wait for further developments.

The garden is still very cold and not very interesting but I do see that we have the first daffodils beginning to show colour. The catkins are beautiful this year and they seem to be very early, but then the 'bread and cheese' (young hawthorn leaves) is appearing in the hedgerows so maybe it will be an early Spring.

The birds are still very busy at the bird tables and it is difficult to keep up with their demands. We fill half coconut shells with any scraps available and set it all in melted suet or fat from the butcher. Suspended upside down from the bird table this is very popular, especially with the tits. We find they prefer this to the fat balls available from the shops.

Daffodils

February 14th, Valentine's Day, is the bird's 'wedding day', so we shall soon see some hectic activity with nest building. We have put up two new nest boxes this year and it will be lovely if they are occupied.

The fieldfares have arrived. We have flocks of them in the field opposite; they make short work of any remaining holly berries. We also have an interesting visitor to the bird table – a stoat or weasel. He is a pretty little thing, but I don't know if I should be encouraging him. I understand they are not too friendly to birds, but he does seem to enjoy the bird fat.

February recipes

Good old-fashioned bread pudding – useful for when you have a smaller first course, equally useful cold at teatime.

GRANDMA'S BREAD PUDDING

350g (12oz) bread, including crusts (not sliced white bread)
75g (3oz) suet   50g (2oz) caster sugar
225g (8oz) mixed dried fruit   1 egg
50g (2oz) flour   1 tablespoon golden syrup
2 level teaspoons mixed spice   demerara sugar

Grease a square 8 inch tin. Cut bread up roughly, put into a basin and saturate with cold water. Leave to soften, then turn into a colander and press out as much of the liquid as possible.

Put bread into a mixing bowl and beat well with a fork. Add suet, sugar, dried fruit, flour, syrup, egg and spice. Mix thoroughly. Turn mixture into prepared tin and smooth top. Sprinkle with a little demerara sugar. Bake in moderate oven 180c, gas mark 4, for about one hour.

Lovely hot or cold!

STUFFED LIVER

225g (½ lb) pigs liver   I chopped onion
I beef cube (made up)   I tablespoon oil cornflour
2 tablespoons sage and onion stuffing (made up as on packet)

Slice the liver, coat with plain flour and fry in oil; place in a greased casserole dish. Put stuffing on top. Fry onion and place on top. Pour stock into pan and thicken with cornflour. Pour over liver, etc., cover and cook slowly for 1½ hours. If gravy is too thick, thin down with water before serving. Serve with vegetables.

FARMHOUSE STICKY GINGER CAKE

100g (4oz) margarine   100g (4oz) sugar
75g (3oz) black treacle   100g (4oz) golden syrup
150ml (¼ pt) milk   I beaten egg
225g (8oz) plain flour   3-4 teaspoons ground ginger
I teaspoon bicarbonate soda

Melt margarine, sugar, treacle and syrup in the milk over a low heat. Cool until lukewarm. Add sieved dry ingredients and beaten egg. Beat well until smooth. Pour into an 8 inch square greased and lined tin. Bake at 150c, gas mark 2, until the cake springs back when pressed gently - about 1½ hours.

This cake is good for freezing. I usually make the whole amount, cut the cake in half when cold and freeze half. Useful for emergencies as it defrosts very quickly.

PINEAPPLE CAKE

150g (6oz) demerara sugar   300g (12oz) mixed fruit
100g (4oz) chopped cherries   100g (4oz) marg
150g (6oz) tinned pineapple (drained and chopped)
6 fl oz juice from the tinned pineapple
225g (8oz) self-raising flour   2 eggs beaten

Mix the first six ingredients together and bring to the boil. Boil
for 10mins and allow to cool. Add the flour and the eggs.
Line a 9 inch cake tin and place mixture into it.
Bake for $1\frac{3}{4}$ hrs at 160c, gas mark 3.

Camellia

Long Tailed Tit

March

'In like a lion and out like a lamb', so the saying goes. So far this year it has been very cold and we have had several falls of snow accompanied by biting easterly winds.

Japanese Quince

We had another egg from Hannah this morning but I don't think Nixie is laying. If she is she is being very secretive about it. There are a lot of pheasants around just now and one in particular visits frequently feeding at the bowls we put out for the geese. He walks with a limp so we know it is the same one. We have named him Frankie and he has become quite friendly.

A pair of blue tits has been showing some interest in one of the new nest boxes and a pair of long tail tits has been visiting the ever busy bird table. They are so pretty with their pink colouring but don't stay for long for us to watch as they are very shy. 'Bobby Dick' still lets all the other birds know he is the boss and the nuthatch is still a regular visitor.

The spring blossoms are so pretty this year and so far the frosts have not spoilt them. Our neighbour has a beautiful mimosa tree out in full flower, a lovely display of yellow fluffy flowers amongst their feathery dark green foliage. The Japanese quince is also in full bloom. I love their pretty cup-like flowers which appear before the leaves and then the apples which follow in the autumn and stay all winter. They seem to be of no interest to the birds. We have five small bushes in the spinney, all grown from seed from an apple from the original shrub and they range in colour from delicate orange to deep cherry. Pink and white camellias and the bright yellow forsythia all play their part in helping us to think spring is on the way. It is the last day of March as I write

Mimosa

this and I am sure something is happening in both the nest boxes. Blue tits have been coming and going so it does look hopeful.

The banks are full of primroses. We cannot let March pass without a record of them. There is so much to do in the garden just now but we must not forget there is still cooking to do!

March recipes

LEMON CURD

4 eggs (use large free range eggs if possible to give a good colour)
4 lemons   450g (1lb) sugar

Beat eggs well and strain through a flour sieve; add sugar and grated rind and juice of lemons. Pour into a basin and place basin over a pan of boiling water. Stir continuously until the mixture thickens. Pot up and seal when cold.

DEVON APPLE CAKE

100g (4oz) caster sugar   100g (4oz) margarine
225g (8oz) self-raising flour (sieved)
1 egg $\frac{1}{2}$ teaspoon vanilla essence
1 apple thinly sliced   milk to mix

Cream margarine and sugar, add beaten egg and vanilla essence. Gradually mix in flour, apple and milk to make a soft dropping mixture. Place in a greased square tin and bake in a moderate oven for about 40 mins. This cake is best eaten on day of cooking. Very good served hot with custard or cream for a sweet.

SHORTBREAD PETTICOAT TAILS

350g (12oz) plain flour   225g (8oz) margarine

75g (3oz) caster sugar   pinch salt

Sift flour into bowl with a pinch of salt; rub in the margarine and, when the mixture resembles breadcrumbs, add 50g (2oz) sugar and knead the mixture into a ball. Cut into two and form each piece into a circle 7 inches in diameter. Flute the edges and place on an ungreased baking tray, marking each piece into 8 pieces, cutting almost through. Bake in quite a low oven 150c-160c, gas mark 2/3, until pale golden. Cool on a wire tray and sprinkle with the remaining sugar. Store in an airtight tin.

BARBARA'S QUICK FRUIT CAKE

100g (4oz) marg

Use a teacup for these measurements:

1 cup demerara sugar   1 1/4 cups mixed fruit

2 cups self-raising flour   1 cup milk

1 tsp mixed spice   2 tsp baking powder

2 eggs beaten   add a small apple if liked

Into a saucepan put marg, sugar, fruit and milk. Heat over a gentle heat until boiling. Cool - about 20 mins. Sieve in flour, spice and baking powder, add beaten eggs and apple, if liked, and mix well. Put into a greased 6 inch cake tin and bake for 1 - 1 1/2 hours at 150c. Turn out when cool on to a wire tray.

ICED FLAPJACKS

125g (5oz) marg   75g (3oz)Demerara sugar
50g (2oz) golden syrup   225g (8oz) porridge oats

Icing - 100g (4oz) icing sugar - 1 tsp coffee - cold water

Melt marg, sugar and syrup in a saucepan over a low heat. Add porridge oats and mix well together and spread in a square greased baking tin. Bake at 200c gas 7 for 20 mins. Ice when cool with the icing sugar ingredients mixed together using as much cold water as needed.

Bluebells. Buttercup Vetch Forget-me-not. Red Campion.

Speedwell.

Clover.

April

April is a lovely month and my flower of this month has to be the magnolia. Its waxy white flowers blushed with pink are magnificent. There is no finer sight than a large magnolia in full bloom. We have the oregan grape also in flower with its bright yellow flowers which last for weeks and the fritillary (snakeshead) so called because of their unusual mauvy pink and spotted markings, are just opening. They do not grow in that many regions so we are lucky they grow here. We keep hoping their numbers will increase. The cowslips in the spinney are out now and look lovely - we are very proud to have grown from seed,

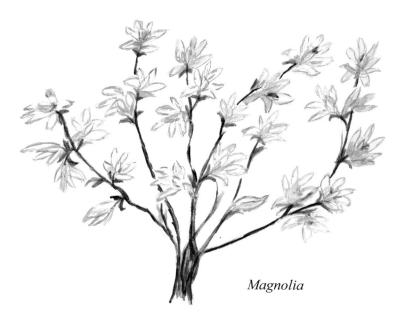

Magnolia

Today we have seen this year's first swallow. We are only a few days into April and this is quite early for them to arrive. 'One swallow does not make a summer', so the saying goes and it is still very cold. We had another frost this morning which will not help the magnolias and camellias and the plum blossom, which is a picture at the moment, will suffer also and will probably affect the eventual crop.

Cowslip

The blue tits are nesting in one of the new nest boxes and we are looking forward to seeing their 'babies' in a few weeks time. Two pairs of chaffinches seem to have made their home around here this year. The males sing so loudly you would think they were in competition with 'Bobby Dick'.

How lovely it is to see the ewes and lambs again in the fields around us, very different to a few years ago when the farms and fields were empty because of the foot and mouth epidemic. Let that never happen again – it was disastrous for so many people and heartbreaking to witness.

The well at last appears to have recovered, but rainfall is still sparse and it is far from being full. We may have a few problems should we have too dry a summer.

Wild Arum

April recipes

DEVON APPLE & DRIED FRUIT FLAPJACK

200g (7oz) porridge oats   25g (1oz) soft brown sugar
90g (3 ½ oz) soft marg   2 tablespoons syrup
2 tablespoons black treacle
75g (3oz) dried fruit (raisins, sultanas, currants)
8 glace cherries quartered   1 apple thinly sliced

Put margarine, syrup, treacle and sugar in a pan and melt. Add oats, fruit and cherries. Stir until all is well coated. Put half of the mixture into a greased 8 inch square tin and press down firmly and evenly. Then put a layer of sliced apple on top, and the remainder of the mixture on top of the apple. Cook for 20-30 mins, oven 190c, gas mark 5. Cut into fingers and remove from tin when cold.

CHOCOLATE CRUMBLE

100g (4oz marg)
1 packet Rich Tea biscuits
2 dessert spn caster sugar
2 tbs golden syrup
4 tsp cocoa

Melt marg, syrup, sugar and cocoa in a saucepan. Crush biscuits with a rolling pin and stir into liquid. Spread in a shallow tin and leave to harden. Cut into squares.

COFFEE AND WALNUT CAKE

225g (8oz) self-raising flour
1/2 tsp salt
2 oz chopped walnuts
2 tbs mil

150g (6oz) marg
150g (6oz) caster sugar
2 eggs beaten.
2 tsp coffee powder

Cream together marg and sugar. Add beaten eggs. Sieve flour and salt and add to mixture with chopped nuts and coffee powder dissolved in the milk.

Put into a greased, lined 7 inch cake tin and bake approx 1 hour at 160c gas mark 4, or until skewer comes out clean.

Ice with coffee icing.

Lily of the Valley

May

W e visited Belstone on Dartmoor today, the gorse is all in flower and there are acres and acres of it, which is very beautiful, but it's encroaching nature and along with the bracken, seems to be taking over. To our great delight we also heard the cuckoo for the first time this year.

The lily of the valley, May's flower of the month, has always been my favourite. I carried it in my wedding bouquet. The delicate white bells hidden amongst strong

Welsh Poppy

dark green leaves and the perfect scent – there is nothing quite like it. The apple blossom in the orchard looks wonderful this year and bodes well for the future crop. Yellow Welsh poppies line the driveway and we have purple and white lilac and golden chain. May is really a lovely month for all the flowers.

There is a prolific show of bluebells and whilst out yesterday we visited a bluebell wood. A beautiful blue sheen, carpets of them as far as we could see. The feeding of the birds through the winter has paid dividends and this morning we have a couple of young robins on the bird table with their little spotty breasts and fluffy bodies they look so cute as they sit there waiting for their parents to show them what to do. Bobby Dick is such a proud dad. We still keep an eye on the bird box to see if any young blue tits emerge. (Next day) Another baby robin, obviously later hatched has appeared this morning – that makes a brood of three – let's hope they all survive. We have also

Periwinkle

seen a brood of three young blackbirds so our bird population has greatly increased

It's ten days now since we first saw the baby robins and they now come to the bird table on their own. Gangly teenagers now, they have lost their round shape and their legs have lengthened.

Hannah the goose has decided at last it's time for a rest and is sitting on nine eggs. She will need to sit for a month so we hope she stays the course.

Bluebells

May recipes

DEVON TEDDIE (POTATO) PIE

900g (2lbs) potatoes
salt and pepper
600ml (1pt) milk
25g (1oz) butter
1 level teaspoon dry mustard (optional)

1 small onion chopped
4 eggs
225g (8oz) grated tasty cheese
salt and pepper

Grease a 3 pint ovenproof dish. Boil potatoes and mash; add salt, pepper, mustard and onion. Line the base and sides of the dish with mashed potato, forking it well up around the sides. Break eggs into a basin and beat them well; add cheese, milk and seasoning. Pour into potato case. Dot with dabs of butter. Bake in a moderate oven for one hour, 160c, gas mark 3. Make half the quantity for two.

GOOSEBERRY JAM

1.4kg (3lbs) gooseberries   600ml (1pt) water
1.4kg (3lbs) sugar

Top and tail gooseberries. Place them in a large pan with the water and bring slowly to the boil. Simmer for about 20 mins. until skins are tender. Add sugar, dissolve, and bring back to the boil for about 15-20 mins. until the mixture sets when tested on a saucer. Pot up and tie down when cold.

Apple Blossom

CHEESEY CHEESECAKES

225g (8oz) self-raising flour   175g (6oz) grated cheese
100g (4oz) marg   1 egg
Salt and pepper   Milk to mix

Rub marg into flour, stir in cheese, salt and pepper and bind together with beaten egg and milk to a stiff consistency. Put into greased bun tins and bake 10-15 mins 180c gas mark 4.

REFRESHER LEMON CAKE

100g (4oz) margarine   175g (6oz) caster sugar

2 beaten eggs   milk

175g (6oz) self-raising flour   50g (2oz) granulated sugar

grated rind and juice of 2 lemons

Cream margarine, caster sugar and lemon rind until fluffy, then beat in the eggs. Mix in flour and about 4 tablespoons milk to make a soft mixture. Grease and line a 900g (2lb) loaf tin and put mixture in, smoothing the top. Bake in a moderate oven, from 180c, gas mark 4, for 45-50 mins. until firm and golden and shrinking from sides of the tin.

Then prepare the lemon syrup by heating the lemon juice and granulated sugar gently until sugar is dissolved. As soon as the cake is removed from the oven, whilst still in the tin, prick all over with a skewer.

Pour the syrup over the cake and leave in the tin until cold.

Rose

June

June is another lovely month and of course the one known for roses. We are now right into summer and we have had some very hot weather, but the last few days have been very wet and cold with some local flooding.

Wild Honeysuckle

The best of the spring blossom is over now but we have the beautiful mauve buddleia alternifolia coming into bloom with its dainty, graceful arching stems – quite different from the usual butterfly bush. The hedgerows along the lane are covered in dog roses and honeysuckle, such a lovely perfume, and the lovely tall spikes of the foxglove are quite spectacular.

The birds are still very busy feeding their young. There are so many around the garden at the moment and they are an attraction for the jackdaws, crows and magpies. I don't like to think why they are so much in evidence but I suppose that is nature and there is nothing we can do about it, but it does seem so very cruel at times. We have several young blue tits in the apple tree which we think were raised in one of our nest boxes. We saw 'the vicar' bathing in the bird bath during the hot spell and although puddles are abundant just now they soon disappear after a few dry days, and I always keep the bird bath topped up with clean water.

We have left our field to grow for hay and whilst walking alongside the hedge the other day I almost trod on a hen pheasant sitting on her nest. I shall watch the nest closely for the youngsters to appear.

I am writing this particular chapter sitting in the summerhouse and there is a mother goldfinch sitting on her nest just a few feet away. The birds are singing, the bees are humming and the sweet peas by the door are filling the air with their perfume.

Foxgloves

We have grown the sweet peas especially this year for our grand daughter's wedding bouquet and posies for the reception tables. They have come into flower at just the right time.

June recipes

COUNTRY FLAN

short-crust pastry
1 onion chopped
1 tablespoon oil
225g (½ lb) cooked chicken,
bacon or any cooked meat
50g (2oz) mushrooms chopped
2 tomatoes chopped
50g (2oz) sweetcorn (either
frozen or tinned)
3 large free range eggs
150ml (¼ pt) milk
50g (2oz) cheese grated
salt and pepper

Siberian Iris

Line a flan dish with short-crust pastry.
Fry the onion in a little oil until soft, then add meat. Stir in mushrooms, tomatoes and sweetcorn. Cook altogether for a few minutes then turn into the pastry case. Beat together the eggs, milk, salt and pepper.
Pour over the mixture and sprinkle with grated cheese. Bake at 180c, gas mark 4, for 30-40 mins or until well set and golden brown. Serve hot or cold.

HASLET

225g (½ lb) liver   225g (½ lb) pork sausage meat
170g pkt sage and onion stuffing mix
pepper to taste   warm water

Chop the liver finely and mix well with sausagemeat and dry stuffing, adding enough warm water to make a soft mixture. Press into a well greased loaf tin and bake for 1½ hours at 180c, gas mark 4. Leave to cool slightly before turning out. Serve cold.

SUMMER PUDDING

900g (2lbs) summer fruit:
raspberries, strawberries,
gooseberries, black & red currants,
rhubarb, or any fruit available
100g (4oz) sugar   little water
several slices of white bread with crusts removed

Cook the fruit in a saucepan with the sugar and a little water until softened but not broken up. Line a 1.2kg (2 pint) pudding basin with slices of white bread, cutting a round for the bottom of the basin. Fill with fruit, then cover the top with bread.

Place a saucer over the basin with a weight on top. Chill in the fridge for several hours. Turn out just before serving and spoon extra fruit over. Serve with pouring cream.

A SUMMERY ELDERFLOWER CORDIAL

1kg (2lbs 2oz) caster sugar
2 lemons sliced
40g (1 1/2 oz) citric acid

900ml (1 1/2 pts) boiling water
15-20 elderflower heads

Put sugar in a large bowl and pour over boiling water, stir to dissolve. Add citric acid and the sliced lemons. Snip off the flower heads (leaving behind the big stalks) and add these. Stir well. Cover with cling film and leave for 5 days, stirring each day. Sieve through muslin into sterile bottles. Dilute to taste.

Keeps well in the fridge, and can be frozen. Lovely to bring out for Christmas. There is such a short time when the flowers are in season, so freezing is the answer. It is a very refreshing drink and a pleasant change from the usual orange or lemon.

DEVON CREAM TEA

225g (8oz) self raising flour
40g (1 1/2 oz) marg
25g (1oz) caster sugar

1 egg
milk to mix
pinch of salt

Rub the margarine into the flour, add salt and sugar. Add beaten egg and milk to make a soft dough. Roll out half inch thick and cut into scones with a pastry cutter. Place on a greased baking sheet. Bake in a hot oven 200c, gas mark 6. Cut in half when cold and serve with strawberry jam and lashings of clotted cream.

July

Red Admiral

J uly and August are traditional holiday months, especially here in Devon. They are also the months when the garden yields lots of salad produce. We have so far enjoyed lettuce, young broad beans, beetroot and new potatoes. However, the garden seems to have been taken over by our bird population and we have had to cover a lot of our young plants with netting – the new green shoots are just too tempting for them.

Peacock

The raspberries, after looking so promising, have been disappointing. Firstly the scorching sun dried up the leaves and then strong winds broke them down. The blackbirds didn't help, they found they could creep under the netting and help themselves. We shall have to devise new means to keep them out next year.

The red currants also fruit this month and I think are always worth growing. Their pretty shiny red berries hang like a string of beads when ripe and they make excellent jelly and wine. We have to cover them with nets again as they are also a favourite with the blackbirds.

The buddleia is blooming now and when the sun shines it is often covered with butterflies. The peacocks and red admirals are so pretty, yet very delicate.

I watched a baby blue tit come to the bird bath today. I had just refilled it with fresh water and it was rather full, but he didn't seem to mind; it came right over his back and he loved it. We have several young swallows around and watching the parent birds encouraging them to fly is a real joy. It's hard to believe that in a few weeks time they will leave and fly thousands of miles to Africa whilst we endure our winter months.

Buddleia

I watched the pheasant in the hayfield sitting on her eggs and a few days ago counted ten empty shells. They have obviously all hatched and moved on – I hope they all survive.

We have an unusual, but very fascinating plant – mirabilis. I think it comes from South America, and it blooms during the evening and at night. We call it our 'moonflower'. It has almost fluorescent white flowers which last for just a short while before turning pink and fading, all within twenty four hours. There can be up to twelve flowers on a plant each evening.

Sweet Pea

July recipes

MOTHER'S DEVON MEAT BALLS

225g (8 ozs) minced beef
100g (4 oz) long grain rice
1 dessertspoon fruit chutney
small tin condensed tomato soup
mixed dried herbs
1 tablespoon oil

40g (1½ oz) fresh breadcrumbs
1 egg
300ml (½ pt) water
flour
salt and pepper

Mix together meat, breadcrumbs, chutney, seasoning and bind with beaten egg. Form into balls and roll in flour. Fry until brown. Place rice in greased casserole dish and put meat balls on top. Heat soup in a saucepan with the water, herbs, salt and pepper.

Pour over the meat balls, making sure you cover all the rice. Cover and bake for 45-60 mins at 170c, gas mark 4.

SUMMER STRAWBERRY GATEAU

3 large eggs
75g (3oz) caster sugar + 2 tablespoons caster sugar
75g (3oz) plain flour
450g (1 lb) strawberries
1 tablespoon hot water
284 ml carton of double cream

Grease and line a swiss roll tin with greaseproof paper. Make sponge by whisking together the eggs, sugar and hot water; fold in the flour. Pour mixture into the prepared tin and smooth. Bake in a hot oven, 200c, gas mark 6 for about 10 mins. Turn out and allow to cool. The sponge can be made beforehand and frozen.

Wash and hull strawberries, cutting in half any large ones. Sprinkle with caster sugar, stir and leave in fridge until needed. Whip the cream until it holds shape. Cut cake in half, spread one half with cream, then strawberries; put the other half on top, then cream and finally the rest of the strawberries. Leave in fridge until needed - one hour or so to settle.

Hardheads, Bird's-foot Trefoil, Wild Poppy, Red Clover, Ox-eye daisy, Field Scabious

TRADITIONAL RED CURRANT JELLY

1.8kg (4lbs) red currants   900ml (1 1/2 pts) water
450g (1lb) sugar to each pint of juice

Wash currants (no need to stalk them). Put in a pan with water and simmer until soft (20 - 30 mins.) stirring and pressing the fruit against the side of the pan to extract as much juice as possible. Pour into a muslin bag and allow to drip. If you squeeze the bag you will get more juice, but it may not be quite so clear. Measure juice and put into pan with the required amount of sugar, then increase heat and boil rapidly for about 15 mins. Test for set. Pour into really hot jars and tie down when cold. Lovely served with roast Devonshire lamb.

BREAD AND CHEESE PUDDING

100g (4oz) stale white bread with crusts
100g (4oz) Double Gloucester cheese
2 spring onions, finely chopped   3 beaten eggs
450ml (3/4 pint) milk   1 teaspoon mustard
4 rashers back bacon   Salt and pepper

Remove rind from bacon and slice in half lengthways. Cut bread into cubes including crusts, place in shallow 2 pint oven-proof dish. Cut cheese into cubes and sprinkle over bread and onions. Beat milk, eggs, mustard, salt and pepper and pour over bread and let soak for 10 minutes. Lay bacon rashers over the top. Bake until golden and crispy for 45 minutes, 200c, gas mark 6. Garnish with chopped fresh parsley and serve with peas.

August

Goldfinch

August does not seem to be a very good month for the birds. After rearing their broods many of them moult and our robin and blackbird are looking decidedly scruffy. Maybe it is nature's way of letting them recover all their energies after all the labour intensive work and effort they have to commit to in bringing up their young. They still come to the bird table so we continue to feed them and they seem to need it.

We had a pair of goldfinches feeding on the thistle seeds today. They are quite beautiful with all their red, yellow and various markings. The sunflowers have now gone to seed and are being greedily attacked by the finches and blue tits.

After the grass was cut in the hayfield we noticed a buzzard keeping close attendance, obviously watching for any prey turned out by the machines. He is spectacular in flight and so graceful.

In the garden we have a super crop of plums, which considering the late frosts we had in the spring, is quite surprising. They will make lovely jams and wine and also freeze well for winter consumption. It is also a good season for tomatoes, a great favourite of mine when picked fresh.

Nasturtum

A few days ago we spent a very pleasant day on Dartmoor although for August it was rather chilly. The heather is at its best just now – a purple sheen as far as the eye could see. We had hoped to see the skylarks but, perhaps because of the cold wind, did not spot a single one.

August recipes

RUNNER BEAN CHUTNEY

900g (2lbs) runner beans (after skinning)
4 or 5 large onions
550g (1¼ lbs) demerara sugar
900ml (1½ pts) vinegar
1½ tablespoons each of
            turmeric, mustard and cornflour

Prepare the beans by slicing, chop the onions and boil together in salted water until tender.

Strain well and chop up small. Put into saucepan and boil with 750ml (1¼ pts) of vinegar and the sugar for 15 mins.

Mix together turmeric, mustard and cornflour with 150ml (¼ pt) vinegar, add to boiling mixture stirring well, and cook for a further 15 mins, making sure it does not stick to the pan.

Pot up in hot jars and leave to cool. Cover when cold. Leave for a few weeks to mature.

Sunflower

PLUM WINE

1.8kg (4lbs) plums
4 cloves
1 lemon (sliced)
25g (1oz) bakers' yeast

6g (1/4 oz) root ginger
4.8 littres (1 gallon) water
1.4kg (3lbs) sugar

Cut up the plums and remove the stones. Bruise the ginger and add to the plums with the cloves and sliced lemon. Pour over 4.8 litres (1 gal) boiling water and stir well. Cover and leave for four days, stirring each day with a wooden or plastic spoon. Strain through muslin onto the sugar, warming a little of the liquid to help the yeast work.

Mix the yeast with a little of the liquid, then add it to the 'wine'. Leave in the pan overnight; next day transfer to a fermentation jar to 'work'. When it has ceased working (after about 3 months), cork the jar, leave for several months before bottling.

Best left a year before drinking.

PLUM JAM

675g (1 1/2 lbs) plums (after stones have been removed)
675g (1 1/2 lbs) sugar
300ml (1/2 pt) water (if plums are firm, less if they are soft)

Cook the plums and water slowly until soft; add sugar and stir over a low heat until dissolved, then boil rapidly until a little tried on a cold plate wrinkles when moved with your finger (about 15 mins). Pot up into hot jars. Cover when cold.

MINCED MEAT AND CHEESE CRUMBLE

1 onion chopped   450g (1lb) minced beef
400g (8oz) tin chopped tomatoes
Salt and pepper   Pinch mixed herbs

Crumble topping: 100g (4oz) plain flour
50g (2oz) marg   50g (2oz) grated cheese

Melt a little oil in a saucepan and fry minced meat and onion until nicely browned. Stir in the tomatoes, salt and pepper and herbs and simmer for 20 mins. The mixture needs to be quite dry so cook a little longer if it is wet. Place in an ovenproof dish. Then make the topping. Rub the marg into the flour, then add the grated cheese. Sprinkle this over the meat mixture. Cook until golden - about 40 mins 180c gas mark 5.

RICH DARK CHOCOLATE OATCAKES

225g (8oz) soft marg   175g (6oz) dark soft brown sugar
225g (8oz) porridge oats   25g (1oz) cocoa powder
225g (8oz) plain dark chocolate

Preheat oven to 180c gas mark 5.
Grease a 7 inch shallow cake tin. Melt marg in a saucepan over a low heat. Remove pan then add sugar, cocoa and oats. Stir the mixture well and put into the cake tin. Bake for about 15 mins until it is bubbling. Allow to cool. Melt the plain chocolate gently in a bowl over a saucepan of hot water, then pour it on top of the cooled oatcake, spreading it flat with a palette knife. Leave in a cool place until set. Cut into squares.

Enjoy!

September

September is the month when the children return to school and the holidays are over and the garden seems to be coming to a close. The remaining produce is almost ready for harvesting and it's time for pickling and preserving. There is a wonderful crop of blackberries this year – they are really plentiful in the hedgerows hereabouts. We have an excellent crop of grapes in the greenhouse. They are so sweet and of a lovely flavour and are surprisingly little trouble to look after.

The farmers' harvest is nearly over now although with the latter part of last month being rather wet it proved a difficult time for them.

Blackberries

The hayfield has been spread with manure and whilst walking across it the other day we picked some lovely field mushrooms. I am very nervous about eating the many edible fungi growing in the hedgerows and banks. Although books assure us there are many which are edible I tend to err on the safe side and admire them for their attractiveness rather than their culinary uses.

The swallows are still around – flying low today which supposedly means rain is on the way. They will soon be lining up on the telephone wires before flying away for winter.

September recipes

MOTHER'S PICCALILLI

1.8kg (4lbs) (prepared weight) cauliflower, runner beans, cucumber, onion, marrow, green tomatoes, or any vegetables of your choice.

1.2 litres (2 pints) vinegar
12g (½ oz) mustard
2 or 3 chillies
salt

12g (½ oz) turmeric
12g (½ oz) ground ginger
100g (¼ lb) brown sugar
2 tablespoons cornflour

Cut the vegetables into small pieces, spread on a large dish, sprinkle well with salt and leave to stand overnight. Next day drain well. Boil together in a large pan the vinegar, turmeric, mustard, ground ginger, chillies and brown sugar, then add the vegetables and simmer for ½ hr. Mix the cornflour with a little of the liquid and add to the mixture, stirring all the time. Cook for a further 15mins., stirring to prevent burning. Pot up and seal with vinegar proof lids. Leave to mature for two months.

CARAMEL SHORTIES
(Something quick and easy for tea!)

100g (4oz) marg
75g (3oz) soft brown sugar

110g (4½ oz) plain flour

Rub marg into flour and sugar. Turn on to a floured board and divide into 18 pieces. Roll each into a ball, flatten slightly. Place on a greased baking tin and bake 15 mins 180c gas mark 4.

HEDGEROW JELLY

900g (2lbs) crab or cooking apples
900g (2lbs) blackberries
1.2 litres (2pts) water
450g (1lb) sugar for each pint of juice

Slice the apples (it is not necessary to peel or core them). Put into a pan with the water and blackberries, and simmer gently until all is a soft pulp. Strain through muslin. If you squeeze the muslin you will get more juice; the experts say you should not do this as it tends to make the jelly cloudy, but I have found no ill-effects from this practice.

Pour juice back into the pan and add sugar. Dissolve over a low heat then bring to a full boil and boil rapidly until the mixture sets when tested on a cold saucer (about 20-30 mins).

Pot up in hot jars and tie down when cold.

Fairy Ring

Field Mushroom

'The Sickener'

APPLE SHORTBREAD

150g (6oz) self-raising flour
100g (4oz) margarine
Pinch salt
75g (3oz) caster sugar

1 egg
450g (1lb) cooking apples
3 level tbs sugar

Cook the prepared and sliced apples and the 3tbs sugar in very little water and allow to cool. Cream margarine and sugar well, stir in beaten egg, flour and salt and leave for a few minutes in the fridge to firm. Grease a deepish 18cm (7inch) tin.

Place two 28cm (11inch) strips of greaseproof paper at right angles across the base and up the sides to enable to be lifted out easily. Then line base and sides with greased greaseproof paper.

Divide mixture into two and roll each piece into an 18cm (7inch) round. Line base of tin with one round, prick it and cover with the cold apple, then place the second round on top and prick lightly. Bake for one hour at 180C gas mark 4.

Geranium.

Mesembryanthemum.

October

We spent a few days in Cornwall at the beginning of October and as we return it is very obvious how autumn has come upon us. The days are very much colder – a keen wind today and the leaves are definitely turning colour and many starting to fall. I walked down the lane today and just noted how many varieties there are here– beech, oak, the pretty field maple and in the spinney hornbeam, alder horse and sweet chestnut, poplar, willow and cherry, all different colours – a lovely sight. The berries on the trees and bushes are also changing colour now.

Beech

English Oak

We have gathered some sweet chestnuts and hazelnuts but the walnuts came to nothing, perhaps the squirrels got to them first. Florescent pink colouring contrasting with the green leaves, particularly on these grey days. The pink and white mini cyclamen are quite a display on the bank and they bloom for a fair time.

Hornbeam

It will soon be harvest festival and as there has been a good crop of apples and vegetables, when displayed along with some chrysanths, it should be able to make a lovely show.

Field Maple

The birds have made their presence known and obviously appreciate the peanut holders we have hung out as they get down to some serious feeding in preparation for the hard months ahead. The swallows have all gone now – here one day, gone the next – instinct tells them when it's time to go.

Wych Elm

We have seen some spectacular rainbows this month. The weather has been very changeable, sunshine interrupted by short sharp showers. It's difficult to recall the order of colours so remember this rhyme: Richard of York gave battle in vain - red, orange, yellow, green, blue, indigo and violet. We have never found the crock of gold at the end of the rainbow, even though it always seems to come down in the spinney. We are still hoping!

Sweet Chestnut

October recipes

WESTCOUNTRY CIDER

1.4kg (3lbs) cooking apples (use windfalls)   900g (2lbs) sugar
7.2 litres (12 pts) cold water   2 large lemons

Ensure the apples are clean and free of maggots, then cut them in pieces with the core and peel. Blast them for a few seconds in the liquidiser (just enough to break them up). Put into a pan and pour over the cold water, stir well, then leave for a week, stirring each day.

At the end of the week strain, then add the sugar and the grated rind and juice of the lemons. Leave for 24 hours. Strain and bottle into glass (not plastic) screw top bottles.

The cider will be ready to drink in a week but better left for two to three weeks.

Warning: Be very steady on opening the bottles as the cider can be very 'lively' - best done in the sink!

Horse Chestnut

AUTUMN TREACLE TART

225g (8oz) short crust pastry
100g (4oz) fresh white breadcrumbs
1 large cooking apple
4 tablespoons golden syrup

Line an 8 inch flan dish with the pastry. Peel, core and slice the apples and place on the pastry. Mix syrup and breadcrumbs together and pour over the apples.
Decorate with pastry trimmings - lattice pattern.
Bake for 45 mins. at 200c, gas mark 6 until golden.

PICKLED MARROW

1 medium sized marrow
75g (3oz) shallots chopped
4 chillies chopped
600ml (1pt) vinegar
50g (2oz) sugar
6g (1/4 oz) turmeric
salt

Peel and cut the marrow into 1 inch wide strips, sprinkle with salt and leave for 24 hours. Strain well. Boil together the shallots, chillies, vinegar, sugar and turmeric for 15 mins. Put in the marrow and simmer a further 10 mins. Pot up and tie down when cold. Very good with baked potatoes and grated cheese.

Nerines

SLOE WINE

This is one of my favourites. Sloes are still to be
found in the lanes and on the moors, but you may
have to look hard to find them.

8 pints sloes   4.8 litres (8pts) boiling water
1.4kg (3lbs) sugar   12g ($\frac{1}{2}$ oz) yeast

Clean the sloes, then put into a large pan. Cover with
boiling water, stir well, cover and leave for four days,
stirring each day. Strain. Then add the previously
activated yeast and the sugar and leave for a
further four days, stirring each day. Pour into a
demi-john, insert an air lock and leave to 'work'.
Rack off when it has stopped working and is clear,
then cork the demi-john and leave for approximately
three months before bottling. This is best left until sloes come
again before drinking.

Willow

CHEESE AND EGG PIE

100g (4oz) Shortcrust pastry 200g (8oz) Cheddar cheese (grated)
4 eggs   25g (1oz) fresh brown breadcrumbs
2 tablespoons milk   salt and pepper and a little butter

Line a 7 inch flan ring or tin with pastry. Place half the cheese
in the case and make four small hollows. Break an egg into each
hollow. Season with salt and pepper. Cover with the rest of the
cheese and breadcrumbs. Dot with butter and moisten all over
with the milk. Bake for 30-45 minutes at 180 c, gas mark 4, until
golden and set. Best served with salad.

November

Stag's horn sumac

We move into November. We have put the clocks back an hour and the days are much shorter. In the garden we are busy tidying up burning the cuttings and scrub. It's time for garden bonfires and general tidying up. We have put the garden 'to bed' for the winter and brought our favourite plants inside. There is a feeling of slowing down. I have a good feeling about November, it's my birthday month and it is rather nice to draw the curtains about teatime and shut out the dark evenings and sometimes nasty weather. We also have the comfort of a lovely log fire.

When the children were much younger we used to so enjoy bonfire night on November 5th. We remember the bonfires at home and the sausage sizzle. Cooking the sausages threaded on to sharpened sticks over the fire,. them falling into the fire and trying to rescue them – they would be cooked black on one side and half raw on the other, but how we all loved it and didn't they taste good, especially on a cold, wet evening. Of course it was all done across the fields and well away from our thatched roofs.

There is very little colour about now but I did pick a beautiful bunch of late roses this morning and we do have a wonderful bank of ferns around the back of the house. It is quite damp and sheltered there and they do seem to enjoy these conditions.

We see the buzzard family circling overhead quite often and 'mewing' to one another. It always strikes me as rather a sad call, but the ultimate this morning was a sparrow hawk landing on the evergreen next to the bird table – obviously waiting for the small birds to come for their breakfast and he was hoping for his. This time he was unlucky, for which I was pleased.

Male Fern

We always attend our Armistice Day services. I think it so important to remember all the lives lost in the Two World Wars and subsequent conflicts.

Christmas is looming up on us far too quickly, so we should start thinking about collecting the ingredients together for the cake and puddings. I never use any wine or spirits in my pudding or cake so to make them a month before is early enough. My pudding recipe I have made every year since we have been married, sometimes under difficult circumstances, but puddings in our family are a tradition. The recipe is my grandmother's and no doubt it was made the same way generations before that.

Large Red Poppies

I wrote down the measurements of the ingredients as my mother put them into the bowl. Previous to this nothing was ever weighed, but the puddings always seemed to come out the same. I am very pleased our daughters are carrying on the tradition.

Hart's-Tongue Fern

GRANDMOTHER'S CHRISTMAS PUDDING

50g (2oz) chopped almonds

2 medium apples (grated, no need to peel)

1 good-sized carrot (grated)

1 orange and 1 lemon (grated peel and juice)

225g (1/2 lb) suet   3 eggs

350g (3/4 lb) demerara sugar   175g (6oz) self-raising flour

225g (1/2 lb) sultanas   125g (1/4 lb) raisins

225g (1/2 lb) currants   50g (2oz) chopped glace cherries

50g (2oz) chopped dates   50g (2oz) chopped peel

1/2 large loaf white breadcrumbs   1/2 teaspoon mixed spice

1/2 teaspoon cinnamon   1/4 teaspoon ground ginger

Mix all the ingredients together in a large bowl, cover and allow to stand overnight. Next day give the mixture a good stir, and don't forget to make your wish! Then comfortably fill the well greased basins. Cover with greaseproof paper and pudding cloths, and gently simmer for 5-6 hours.

When required for use cook for a further 1 1/2 hours. Serve with a sprinkling of caster sugar, custard or cream.

The above quantity will make approximately four one pint puddings.

CHRISTMAS CAKE

This is my Christmas cake recipe, taken many years ago from the probably long forgotten 'Daily Sketch' newspaper (with a few alterations), but a very trustworthy recipe.

350g (12oz) self-raising flour

pinch salt

150g (5oz) butter

1 tablespoon black treacle

100g (4oz) chopped glace cherries

450g (1lb) sultanas

100g (4oz) raisins

6g (1/4 oz) mixed spice

6 eggs

150g (5oz) margarine

275g (10oz) caster sugar

50g (2oz) chopped almonds

50g (2oz) mixed peel

450g (1lb) currants

100g (4oz) chopped dates

grated rind & juice of
   1 orange and 1 lemon

Cream fat and sugar, add beaten eggs and all the other ingredients and mix to a fairly stiff consistency. Line a 10 inch cake tin with double greased greaseproof paper and put in the mixture, smoothing out the top. In addition to lining the tin I always tie a sheet of brown paper around the outside of the tin as a precaution; this stops the cake from drying out too much in the cooking.

Cook for 2 hours at 180c, gas mark 4, then reduce oven to 150c, gas mark 2 for a further 2 to 2 1/2 hours. Test with a skewer to see if it is cooked. Allow to cool slightly, then turn out to cool on a wire tray.

Store in a tin until you are ready to ice. About a week before Christmas cover top and sides with marzipan and royal icing.

DEVON CIDER CAKE

225g (8oz) mixed sultanas, currant and raisins
4 tablespoons sweet cider   175g (6oz) butter or margarine
175g (6oz) soft brown sugar   3 eggs
225g (8oz) self-raising flour   1 teaspoon mixed spice

Soak the fruit in cider overnight. Cream butter and sugar and add the beaten eggs. Mix in the fruit and cider, then fold in the flour and mixed spice. Place in a greased and lined 8 inch round cake tin and bake in a moderate oven, 180c, gas mark 4 for about 1 hour 10mins. Test with a skewer. Turn out onto a wire tray when cooled slightly.

APRICOT OAT CRUNCHIES

75g (3oz) self-raising wholemeal flour
75g (3oz) porridge oats   75g (3oz) granulated sugar
100g (4oz) marg   100g dried apricots soaked overnight

Grease a swiss roll tin.
In a bowl mix together flour, oats and sugar. Rub in marg until the mixture resembles breadcrumbs. Spread half the mixture over the tin and press down well. Drain and chop the apricots and sprinkle them over the mixture in the tin. Spread over the remaining mixture and press down well. Bake 25 mins 180c gas mark 4. Leave in tin to cool and then cut into 12 pieces.

December

We cleaned out the nest boxes today which we put up last spring and what a lovely surprise to find they had both been occupied during the spring and summer. No doubt the young blue tits we saw around back in the summer had been the occupants. Now they have clean beds for next year. We are intending to put out robin and wren boxes for next season.

The garden has turned full circle and the jasmine and lily of the valley bush are in full flower once again and the holly trees are covered in berries. We hope the birds have left us just enough for our Christmas decorations.

The ivy is really making a show this year and we have mistletoe growing on an apple tree in the spinney. It has grown from a berry which we pushed into the bark of the tree many years ago, but as of yet has never berried.

Dec 19th. We had an awful lot of rainfall last night and today what a surprise to wake to a layer of snow – it's very pretty – just a little early for Christmas Day.

Dec 25th. Christmas day and yes we have snow again. The weatherman said we would and he was right. It settled and the children loved it. The birds are extra busy and because it's Christmas we make sure all the feeders are full and how they appreciate it.

Holly

DEVON WINTER ROOT BAKE

350g (12oz) parsnips
350g (12oz) Devon swede
1/2 small tub soured cream (70 ml)
1 level dessertspoon chopped thyme leaves
1 level tablespoon hot horseradish
salt and pepper

Topping
50g (2oz) butter
1 small onion chopped finely
50g (2oz) fresh white breadcrumbs
25g (1oz) grated Parmesan cheese
1 level dessertspoon chopped thyme leaves

Peel parsnips and swede and chop. Boil in salted water until tender. Drain well, mash together until smooth, but still with a bit of texture. Stir in cream, horseradish and thyme. Season with salt and pepper. Spoon into greased shallow ovenproof dish, and set aside.

Melt butter in frying pan and fry onion for 5 - 6 mins until really golden. Mix in breadcrumbs and stir over low heat to brown and crisp a little. Season and add thyme. Scatter over the mashed vegetables and sprinkle Parmesan over the top.

It may be kept covered in the fridge at this point for up to a day or frozen for up to one month. Bake at 190c, gas mark 5, for 25-30 mins if just made, or 35-40 mins if from cold, until golden and crisp on top.

EMERGENCY BREAD

A useful recipe should you run out of bread
over the holiday or at a weekend.

225g (8oz) plain flour   4 level tsp baking powder
1 level tsp salt   Approx 0.15 litres (1/4 pt) milk and water mixed

Mix flour, baking powder and salt in a bowl. Gradually stir in liquid
until you have a soft spongy dough. Turn on to a floured board
and knead quickly into a round flat loaf. Place on a greased baking
sheet and bake for 45mins 200c gas mark 6 until golden and
sounds hollow when tapped underneath.

NUTTY TOFFEE CRUNCH

90g (3 1/2 oz) mixed nuts   90g (3 1/2 oz) caster sugar
60ml (2 fluid oz) water

Roast the nuts under the grill until just brown. Into a heavy
based saucepan put sugar and water and heat slowly without
stirring until the sugar is dissolved. Bring to the boil then tip in
the nuts and boil rapidly until mixture turns a rich brown colour.
Tip quickly onto an oiled baking sheet and leave to set. When cold,
break into pieces and store in an airtight container.

GOLDEN DATE AND CARROT CAKE

175g (6ozs) dates chopped   175g (6ozs) marg
175g (6ozs) demerara sugar   75g (3ozs) golden syrup
350g (10ozs) self-raising flour   Pinch of salt
3 eggs   2 level tsp ground cinnamon
225g (8ozs) finely grated carrots 2 rounded tbs demerara sugar

In a saucepan melt slowly the marg, 175g (6ozs) sugar and syrup. Remove from heat and sift into the pan the flour, salt, cinnamon and mix well. Beat eggs and add. Stir in the dates and carrots. Pour mixture into an 8inch square greased and lined cake tin. Sprinkle over the 2tbs demerara sugar.
Bake at 160c gas mark 3 for 1 hour 40 mins. Test with a skewer when cake shrinks from the sides of the tin. Leave to cool in tin. Turn out and wrap in foil for 3-4 days to mature.

Mistletoe

New Year's Eve

'Bobby Dick', our faithful robin is back on the bird table. I like to think it is the same one which we have fed, watched and enjoyed all year through, but I doubt it. A robin's life span is very short. If it's not 'Bobby Dick' maybe it's one of his offspring which he brought to the bird table as a fledgling.

On the ground beneath the bird table the 'vicar' busily picks at the scraps and pecks at the apple slices we have thrown there for him. With his distinctive white collar we know this is our 'special' blackbird. Let's hope they continue to grace us with their presence over the next twelve months as we look forward to another year in the garden and kitchen.